Allies for Justice

How Louis Redding and Collins Seitz Changed the Complexion of America's Schools

~

Kathleen Marie Doyle

PublishAmerica
Baltimore

All royalties from the sale of this book are donated to the Community Legal Aid Society, Incorporated.

First printing

ISBN: 1-60441-072-8
PUBLISHED BY PUBLISHAMERICA, LLLP
www.publishamerica.com
Baltimore

Allies for Justice

How Louis Redding and Collins Seitz Changed the Complexion of America's Schools

~

Kathleen Marie Doyle

Dedication

This book is dedicated to my students, past and present.

Acknowledgements

My husband, James G. McGiffin, Jr., staff attorney for the Community Legal Aid Society (co-founded by Collins Seitz) was my inspiration and number one research assistant for this book. The work that Legal Aid does on behalf of those in need is a constant reminder that America still has a distance to go before achieving its ideals. Our teenagers, Bridget and Conor, served as proofreaders and cheerleaders. The Seitz family gave support and enthusiasm to this project even amidst 50th anniversary (of the *Brown* decision) celebrations and a constant barrage of requests from individuals and organizations throughout the country. The Chancellor's wife, Mrs. Virginia Seitz graciously granted an interview. His sister, Dr. Margaret Seitz, the family's historian provided photographs and an interview. C.J. Seitz, Jr. provided boxes and boxes of his father's documents and photos for my perusal, and his secretary, Shirley Jones was delightfully generous with her assistance. Virginia "Muffy" Seitz, the Chancellor's daughter, shared a number of personal documents, including the eulogy which she presented at her father's funeral.

Tom Summers from the Delaware Public Archives helped find a number of resources, and his own knowledge is truly encyclopedic. Leland Ware, the Redding Chair at the University of Delaware gave me direction in my Redding research, including introducing me to the work of Annette Woolard-Provine whose research on the Redding family is both thorough and fascinating. Celia Cohen's research also greatly enriched my understanding of Delaware politics. Thanks also to Ed Kee for his research and presentations about desegregation in Delaware, and Pat Quann for the resources of the Delaware Law Related Education Center. I am also grateful for the help and patience of Rebecca Baird from the Delaware State Bar Association, Lisa Gensel from the University of Delaware's Archives, Anne Haslam, the chief librarian at *The News Journal,* and Gayle Lynch from Brown University's Archives. A truly special thanks goes to Christine Retz, managing editor from Associated University Presses who held my hand through cyberspace throughout much of this production. My colleagues, Michelle Brymer, Lynn Edler, Chris Steele and Tom Zolper, gave generous assistance and feedback. And finally, thanks to Sandra Baker, Loretta Burdette, Janis Cadel and Dustin Putman from PublishAmerica for their faith, patience and guidance.

Chapter 1: From Civil War to Civil Rights

We hold these truths to be self-evident, that all men are created equal, that they are endowed by their Creator with certain unalienable Rights, that among these are life, Liberty and the pursuit of Happiness.—That to secure these rights, Governments are instituted among Men, deriving their just powers from the consent of the governed—That whenever any Form of Government becomes destructive of these ends, it is the Right of the People to alter or to abolish it, and to institute new Government, laying its foundation on such principles and organizing its powers in such form, as to them shall seem most likely to effect their Safety and Happiness.

—Declaration of Independence, 1776

The year was 1951. The young judge, Collins Seitz, listened intently as Louis Redding presented the case. Seitz recognized that any decision he made had the potential to radically change the lives of many communities and many more children. The fundamental question that Seitz needed to answer was one of the most profound legal questions of America's twentieth century: Did the United States Constitution require black children to go to separate schools from white children?

If Louis Redding won this case, it would be the first real victory for black children in the nation's history. As Delaware's only African American attorney for over twenty-five years, he understood the humiliation of segregation. He knew he had to win.

Redding called his next witness to the stand, Dr. Frederic Wertham, a world renowned psychiatrist. He asked Dr. Wertham to share his findings with the Court. Dr. Wertham turned to the judge and explained that even if these children had a beautiful school with "marble halls" and Albert Einstein as their teacher, the fact that the law stated they were forbidden to learn alongside white children was by itself "anti-educational." The children, according to Dr. Wertham, saw segregation "as punishment." (1)

Chancellor Seitz sat expressionless. Outside the courtroom, he smiled easily. His smile began with his eyes, gradually pulling his entire face into a cheerful grin. But inside the courtroom, no one could ever tell what he was thinking. He was called "the Great Stone Face." (2) But his mind was busy weighing the evidence. His job required him to apply the law to all cases. But what if the law were unjust? The psychiatrist testified persuasively that keeping children separated because of their race created lasting and harmful effects on all the children involved. Because of segregation, black children believed they were inferior to white children, and white children also believed black children were inferior. After all, white children had nicer schools, shorter distances to travel, and they even had school busses. Black children had none of these.

Seitz decided to visit the schools to do his own comparison. In 1951, there were only three high schools for African Americans in the entire state of Delaware, and most black children had to provide their own transportation. At Howard High School, in northern Delaware, while most of the teachers were highly qualified, they were paid much less than their white colleagues and Howard's classrooms were packed tightly with children. The children had outdated, used textbooks, and second-hand pencils, too worn down to fit into a pencil sharpener. The black schools were not equal to the white schools.

The Chancellor recognized the injustice of segregation. In fact, he had been making speeches against racism for several years. He recognized that even in the rare circumstance when black students had a nicer school than white students, segregation created lasting psychological effects.

Yet, what could he do about it? These kinds of cases were

challenging judges all over the country. Seitz was passionate about the law, but he knew it was not his job to change the law. He was a state judge. It was his job to make sure the law was carried out with fairness. He deeply respected the United States' system of government which divided political power into three branches and left certain duties to the states. The Supreme Court of the United States upheld segregation fifty-five years earlier and the Supreme Court rarely changed its mind over decisions it had made in the past.

Seitz wondered how the Supreme Court could have decided in 1896 that separating the races in public places was something the founding fathers intended when they wrote the Constitution. That 1896 case, known as *Plessy versus Ferguson*, involved Homer Plessy, who wanted to ride in the "white" section of the train. Since one of his great grandparents had been black, he was ordered to sit in the "colored" section. He refused, was arrested, and he took his case to court. The Supreme Court decided that the founding fathers would not have wanted anyone's political rights denied, but that the Constitution did not require social interaction between the races. They wrote that as long as public facilities for the two races were equal, separating the races socially did not violate the Constitution. The ruling established what came to be known as the "separate but equal" doctrine.

The Civil War had ended over thirty years before the Plessy case, and many people believed that racism and discrimination would end when slavery ended. The war lasted four years, and left a division that is still sometimes apparent in parts of the north and the south. Delaware, the home of Louis Redding and Collins Seitz, lies right in the middle of the north and the south, on the East Coast in the Mid-Atlantic. Its one hundred mile length is divided into three counties. The northernmost county, New Castle County with its lovely rolling hills, had many "northern" characteristics. New Castle County became an industrial center due to the work of immigrants like the DuPonts who settled there. The two southern counties, Kent and Sussex, were flat and agricultural. The further south in Delaware that one traveled in the early 1800s, the more slaves one encountered.

During the Civil War, Delaware was a "border state," remaining with the Union while also remaining a slave state. Generally, because Delaware held slaves and because the state put some of the nation's strictest segregation laws into place following the Civil War, Delaware shared more of its regional identity with the south than with the north. Historians generally refer to Delaware as a southern state.

The most pressing tasks following the Civil War included rebuilding the south (the era known as "Reconstruction"), and finding ways to help the newly freed slaves as they made their transition from plantation life to employed life. For a brief period, options seemed unlimited. Many black colleges were created during this time. The federal government passed the Thirteenth, Fourteenth and Fifteenth Amendments, sometimes referred to as the Civil War or Civil Rights Amendments. The Thirteenth Amendment officially freed the slaves, and the Fifteenth Amendment granted black men the right to vote. The Fourteenth Amendment was the part of the Constitution that would become so significant in the cases argued by Louis Redding and decided by Collins Seitz.

The Fourteenth Amendment has several components. First, it defines a citizen as anyone born in America. This formally recognized that former slaves were citizens—whereas before the Civil War, slaves were treated as property, without rights. The Fourteenth Amendment also declares that states cannot deprive people of equal protection of the law (the Equal Protection Clause). In addition, the amendment states that the government must respect all of a person's legal rights and guarantee basic fairness in legal proceedings (Due Process). Redding focused his arguments on the Equal Protection Clause of the Fourteenth Amendment.

As southern states were "forgiven" and re-entered political life after the Civil War, state governments began putting up obstacles to the freedoms that African Americans had so briefly enjoyed shortly following the Civil War. For example, people had to pay a tax if they wanted to vote. These taxes were called "poll taxes." Poor people could not afford to pay the tax and most blacks were very poor. People also had to take a literacy test if they wanted to vote. People who could not read were barred from voting. Since learning to read was illegal in times of slavery, most recently freed blacks were illiterate, and therefore could not vote. Poll taxes and literacy tests also had the effect of keeping people who were sympathetic to African Americans' plight out of elected office.

As time went on, public facilities including transportation and education became increasingly segregated. Homer Plessy believed separate cars on trains went against the spirit of the Constitution. The Supreme Court of the United State disagreed with him. Segregated facilities became the law of the land. Once a decision is made by the Supreme Court, it is almost impossible to reverse it. Overturning the Plessy decision became Louis Redding's quest and Collins Seitz's dilemma.

Chapter 2:
Lawyer Redding

The Redding name would be associated with profound changes in law and society in Delaware and the nation." (1)

When Louis Lorenzo Redding was growing up in the early part of the 1900's, he was not allowed to play on the same playground with white children, to drink from the same water fountains, to sit wherever he wanted in the movie theater, or to go to the school nearest to his home if white children attended the school. Segregation was the law of the state of Delaware.

Over a century after the Declaration of Independence had declared that it was obvious that all men were created equal, the laws in the United States made it clear that somewhere along our journey toward democracy, we made a wrong turn. The laws in our land suggested that all men were NOT created equal.

Louis was born on October 25, 1901 to two of the most highly educated African Americans in Wilmington, Delaware. His father, Lewis, was the son of a slave. Mr. Redding managed to work his way through college and graduate from Howard University in 1897 at the age of thirty.

Louis's mother, Mary Ann Holmes, came from wealth. Most African Americans in the south were slaves before the Civil War, but not the Holmes. Mary Ann's parents were free Virginians. Mary Ann also attended Howard University, but left the year after she met Lewis. Lewis hoped to marry Mary Ann right away, but her parents disapproved of Lewis's background, and forbade her to marry until they waited for a while and until Lewis had earned and saved enough money. These two children of very different backgrounds married in June of 1900 and moved to Wilmington, Delaware to open a small grocery store.

The grocery store failed after three years. The community was quite poor, and Lewis allowed many of his clients to buy on credit. Many were too poor to ever pay him. Mary Ann was very unhappy in Wilmington. African Americans were only allowed to live on the East Side, which was home to factory pollution, flooding, poverty, deteriorating housing and disease. Mary Ann's mother refused to visit them. When Mary Ann was pregnant with Louis, she returned to Virginia to give birth.

Lewis eventually landed a job as a postal carrier, which was a secure and reasonably well-paying job. He also worked several part-time jobs as his family grew. He worked for local caterers and brought home goodies for the children. In the summer, he worked as a farm-hand on weekends. Lewis planned to send his five children to college, and these jobs would help him to make that happen. Lewis's hard work eventually made it possible for the Redding family to move into the neighborhood that lay just on the outskirts of the poor East Side. The new neighborhood had been predominantly white, and within a few years, became the neighborhood for Wilmington's black middle class.

Mary Ann gave birth to six more children after Louis, but two died in infancy. She stayed at home to raise her children. She taught them at home in their early grades. Even though Louis was two years older than Gwendolyn, their mother enrolled them in third grade together at Howard school. A great deal of attention and expectation was placed on the two oldest children. Their parents referred to them as "Brother" and "Sister," as did their younger siblings. (2)

The Redding family attended Bethel African Methodist Episcopal (A.M.E.) church, one of the city's oldest congregations, which was formal and conservative. The Redding parents were very devoted to their church and their faith. The Redding children were expected to attend church, and they were not allowed to go to the movies or the theater.

The Redding home was strict and disciplined, yet warm. The children called their parents, "Papa" and "Mama", with the accent on the second syllable. (3) When the family gathered for meals, everyone got on their knees first to say grace. The children recalled that these prayers of thanksgiving seemed very long. Even though the elegant Redding family ate their meals on fine china, mealtimes were relaxing moments in each day. Papa's booming laughter sometimes interrupted the enthusiastic conversations about school and current events.

Lewis Redding helped found the Wilmington branch of the National Association for the Advancement of Colored People (NAACP) in 1914. The NAACP was created to promote pride within the black community and to attack segregation. Lewis also pushed for a YMCA for the black community as black children had few places where they could play in Wilmington. They were not allowed on most playgrounds, and their schools had no gym or playing fields. Lewis was devoted to Delaware, and committed to improving life for African Americans in his community. His devotion and commitment rubbed off on his children. All of his children learned these lessons and went on to become well-known for their leadership and commitment to people's rights.

When young Louis reached high school age, the only black public high school in the state, was Howard. In fact, when Louis and Gwendolyn attended school, Howard was the only black school in Wilmington, housing all grades.

Louis was fortunate because he lived close enough to walk. Students who lived too far to walk had to find their own rides to Howard, because even though the state of Delaware provided and paid for the school busses that white students rode to school, black students had to find their own way to school. Black parents had to pay for transportation, give their receipts to the state, and then the state would refund their money. Most parents could not afford to pay that much money up front. Most African Americans therefore, were unable to go to high school in Louis's time.

Howard school was under-funded and overcrowded. Children of

various ages learned in the same classroom. The school had no library. Science classes had no science labs. Teachers donated their own books. Howard had a limited number of extracurricular activities and few sports teams because the school did not have a gymnasium. Team uniforms were costly and without school busses, the school had no transportation for students to compete away from home. Howard did not even have its own athletic field nearby. Textbooks and other resources were hand-me-downs from area white schools. Louis hated this arrangement and said the used books made him feel "second fiddle." (4)

Even though the school had inadequate funding and was overcrowded, Howard attracted some of the most highly educated African American teachers in the country, and the school was renowned for its quality education. Most schools in Delaware, black or white, did not come close to offering the same quality of education at that time. In fact, by 1919, Delaware had one of the worst education systems in the nation. Delaware's General Assembly did not value public education, and children were only expected to attend school for three months out of the year. Delaware was an agricultural state, and children were expected to be available to work on the farms.

By the 1920's, P.S. DuPont, a wealthy industrialist and philanthropist, had become so frustrated with the state's lack of concern for education, he donated six million dollars of his own money to build schools. He donated his money for white schools and black schools. DuPont gave enough money to build eighty-nine black schools, including a new Howard High School, which was built in 1928. The new Howard was a state-of-the-art high school, with science labs, a library, and a gym—easily the finest high school for African Americans in the Middle Atlantic region. Unfortunately, the school was built in the East Side between two animal tanning factories. When the weather was warm, and the windows were open, the stench was repulsive. The smell even seeped through closed windows during the winter.

Louis was highly intelligent and had learned everything that he could at Howard, but he had become bored. By his senior year, the work was no longer challenging. He was eager to move on. Not only was he ready to tackle higher level academics, he hated the race restrictions in his hometown and was looking forward to change. Many places were off-limits to him because he was black. These segregation laws, known as "Jim Crow" laws, angered him. He could not wait to leave Delaware behind. He was ready to explore new places.

Louis and his sister Gwendolyn had always been in the same class and their parents wanted the two siblings to stay together. Brown University admitted Louis and gave him a partial scholarship. Pembroke, Brown's sister school, accepted Gwendolyn. Both universities were highly competitive, only accepting the highest achieving students in the nation. Louis was the first graduate of Howard High School to be accepted into Brown, and Gwendolyn was the first to attend Pembroke. Many members of the community went to the train station to see the two siblings off. Friends and family cheered and applauded as Louis and Gwendolyn boarded the train to Providence, Rhode Island.

Louis was very happy at Brown. Even though the minority population was tiny, the lack of minorities did not bother him. He loved the intellectual stimulation of the campus, and his professors noticed his abilities. He was thrilled that Jim Crow laws did not exist in Rhode Island and the general freedom to come and go as he pleased gave him great joy.

Brown was not perfect, however. No fraternities accepted minority students, and when Louis worked to establish a black fraternity, the university told him that the campus already had enough fraternities. Louis decided if he could not create a fraternity on campus, he would set up a fraternity off campus, in the city of Providence. A small group of black students, including Louis, along with several local black businessmen successfully established a chapter of Alpha-Phi-Alpha. Louis developed a busy social life within that setting.

Gwendolyn was unhappy in Providence. She was the only African American at Pembroke, which made her uncomfortable. To make matters worse, she and Louis shared an apartment, and Louis expected her to do all the cooking and cleaning! She and Louis were separated for the first time in their lives during their sophomore year, when she transferred to her parents' alma mater, Howard University, in Washington, D.C.

Louis went to Brown thinking he wanted to be a doctor. The field of medicine was open to African Americans and Wilmington had several black doctors. As he furthered his studies, however, he discovered that he was much more interested in the law than medicine. He met several black attorneys while he was at Brown, and he liked their lifestyles. He particularly liked how they dressed. He adopted their fashion as his own, wearing Brooks Brothers suits and expensive shoes. He also started smoking English cigarettes. The more he thought about it, the more he realized his skills were a good match for the legal profession. He was an excellent speaker, and earned much recognition for his skill. He graduated from Brown in 1923, and he won the university's award for distinguished oratory. He was selected to speak at the graduation ceremony.

Louis hoped to begin law school right away, but his father had other plans for him. Each of the Redding children contributed to their education by working full-time during the summers and part-time while at school. Louis worked for a catering service in Providence, and earned spending money and free meals. When he graduated from Brown, his father expected him to work in order to contribute to the education fund of the younger siblings, and in order to save for his own graduate work. Louis worked for two years, first as an assistant principal at a school in Florida and then as an English teacher in Atlanta, Georgia.

Louis Redding's Brown University yearbook photo, 1923.
Courtesy of Brown University Archives

During these two years of working, Louis researched law schools. Law schools were generally segregated, and the best law school for African Americans was Howard University Law School. There were several predominantly white institutions which accepted black students, and he looked into those as well. He settled upon one of the most highly respected law schools in the nation, Harvard Law School. He was the second African American to graduate from Harvard Law.

Louis fantasized about becoming a highly paid, well dressed New England lawyer, like many of the friends he met while at Brown. There were no black attorneys in Delaware and he was not eager to return to Jim Crow after the freedom he had enjoyed up north. Louis's father, however, wanted his son to return to Wilmington to challenge Jim Crow laws. Louis dutifully returned to Delaware.

Chapter 3: Delaware's First Black Attorney

How can you boast about being the first when you realize it was the result of racism and apathy? —Louis Redding (1)

After he finished law school, Louis returned to Delaware, at his father's request. He had to do much more than simply graduate from law school, however, if he wanted to practice law in Delaware. Delaware required new attorneys to have a preceptor—an experienced attorney who mentors new attorneys for one year. Louis needed to find a preceptor and he needed to pass the bar exam.

Louis wasn't concerned about the exam, but he was concerned about the preceptorship. White attorneys refused to mentor black attorneys. The preceptorship was the legal requirement which had kept any black attorney from practicing in the state. No one really knows for certain why Judge Daniel O. Hastings agreed to be Louis's preceptor, except that Hastings intended to run for the United States Senate, and he needed the black vote. Some sources say Louis's father agreed to campaign for Hastings in return for a preceptorship for his son. Hastings ran for the Senate in 1928, received black support and won the election.

Louis was humiliated by this arrangement and believed that Hastings was dishonest. He was afraid his involvement with Hastings would hurt his reputation. In fact, Hastings was not the least bit interested in mentoring Louis. He gave Louis a desk in a hallway, but told him not to use it. Louis spent most of the year working out of the Wilmington Law Library.

On March 19, 1929, Louis was sworn in before the state bench. For the next twenty-five years, Louis was the only black attorney in Delaware. Chief Justice James Pennewell said to Louis, "Young man, I hope that by your conduct as a lawyer, you will justify your admission today." (2) The Chief Justice need not have worried.

Louis immediately set to work on challenging segregation in the courtroom. While he was still in law school, he came home for Christmas break, and wanted to observe a hearing at the Municipal Court. The Court required blacks and whites to sit on separate sides of the courtroom. Louis sat on the white side and was kicked out of the courtroom. As soon as he became a lawyer, he wrote an angry letter to his former preceptor, Judge Hastings. Louis challenged the practice of segregation and argued that there wasn't even a law requiring it. Shortly thereafter, segregated seating in Wilmington's courts came to an end.

Louis was lonely and frustrated as the only black lawyer in Delaware. Most judges and other attorneys simply avoided him, but some were blatantly rude to him. The private clubs where many attorneys socialized did not admit African Americans. Even the Delaware State Bar Association, the professional organization which provides services and benefits to Delaware lawyers, excluded blacks. Once, a bailiff tried to throw Louis out of the courtroom because he didn't believe Louis was an attorney.

The early years were difficult for Louis. He handled many cases that other attorneys would not take, and these cases were often lost causes. Clients who had money did not hire Louis, because even if they had faith in his ability, they believed that racist judges would automatically rule against a black attorney. In the 1930's, as unemployment grew and the economy collapsed in the Great Depression, Louis's case load increased dramatically. His fees were lower than other attorneys which meant that people could afford to hire him more easily than other attorneys. While he still was not making a lot of money, he was working on a wider variety of cases and winning. People around town began calling him "Lawyer Redding."

Louis was considered one of the most eligible bachelors in town. He enjoyed courting a number of women. He was handsome, his dress was impeccable, and he enjoyed expensive English cigarettes (although he typically left them unlit). He did not seem very interested in the idea of marriage. He spent many years coming and going as he pleased, and most of his waking hours were devoted to his work. But, in April, 1944, at the age of 43, Louis married Ruth Cook. Ruth didn't believe Louis would go through with the wedding, until he actually showed up at the church.

Ruth graduated from the Philadelphia College of Osteopathy in 1937, and was fifteen years younger than Louis. They each respected one another's intelligence, and allowed each other a great deal of freedom—in fact, they spent much of their marriage apart. Ruth spent time in London studying. Louis often only came home on weekends when they lived in New Jersey and he worked in Wilmington. After twenty-five years of marriage, and raising three daughters, they accepted the fact that they had never quite figured out how to live as a married couple and they called it quits. They remained good friends. Louis remarried in 1972 at the age of 71.

Over time, judges and attorneys grew to respect Louis's skills as an attorney. He was always meticulously prepared. When he spoke, he was precise and commanding. His writing was clear and exact. Although he was only 5'6", his presence filled the room. His clothing was elegant, and he carried himself calmly with stoic dignity. Some people viewed him as cold and indifferent. He revealed his emotions only to those closest to him. He had a slight hearing impairment which may have been one reason he did not spend much time engaging in small talk.

Early in his legal career, he became an active member of the National Association for the Advancement of Colored People. In the mid-1930's, the NAACP developed a legal strategy to attack Jim Crow laws in education, school by school, state by state. The leader of this attack was Charles Houston, the first African American to graduate from Harvard Law School. The law stated that "separate" should be "equal," and the legal team of the NAACP decided to begin their attack by demanding equal facilities rather than integrated facilities. As these cases grew, states either struggled to find the money to build separate but equal facilities, or more likely, simply stalled. By the mid-1940's, the NAACP altered their direction and began to directly attack the law itself, arguing that segregation violated the Fourteenth Amendment's equal protection and due process guarantees, and therefore was unconstitutional.

Louis Redding began the attack in Delaware.

Chapter 4: Collins Seitz

"They called us 'dirty Catholics' but his usual response was, 'I may be Catholic, but I'm not dirty'."—Margaret Seitz, about her brother Collins

Collins Jacques Seitz was born on June 20, 1914, the fifth son in a row for George and Margaret Seitz. A daughter followed six years later. They lived in Forty Acres, a lower-middle class neighborhood, home to many of Wilmington's Irish Catholics. The Ku Klux Klan was active in this part of the state, and they hated African Americans, Catholics and Jews.

When Collins was five, the family moved from the city to a more well-to-do neighborhood just on the border of the city. They were the first Catholic family to move into this mostly Methodist, all white neighborhood and many of the neighbors were dismayed by their arrival and would not let their children play with Collins and his siblings. He grew up hearing taunts of "dirty Catholics" and his usual response was, "I may be Catholic, but I'm not dirty." (1)

Collins always viewed himself as somewhat of an "underdog," and said in later years, that he decided to go into law because he was "always for the underdog." (2) His early experiences with anti-Catholic prejudice may have had something to do with this view that he had of himself. Collins' four older brothers enjoyed teasing their youngest brother, and Collins later mused that these experiences left him with a deep revulsion for injustice. The boys left their baby sister Margaret alone, sparing her the treatment they heaped on Collins.

Collins' sense of fairness may have also been passed down through his family tree. His father was George Seitz, a DuPont employee, and his father's father was Jacques Seitz who came to the United States in 1870 from Alsace. Jacques decided to move to America rather than submit to the Germans when they took over the Alsace region of France. He found a job working for the DuPonts who were also French.

Jacques married Anna Gibbons, who also worked for the DuPonts, as did many Irish Americans, including Anna's father. Collins commented many years later, that the Irish "were expendable because a lot of the Irish were killed in the powder works explosion." (3)

Collins' mother was Margaret Collins. Margaret's mother's family descended from Quakers, and her family was an old Delaware family who had fought in the Revolutionary War. The Quakers were very socially active, and led the movement to abolish slavery before the Civil War.

Collins' mother, Margaret, gave birth to nine children at home. Three of them died in infancy. Collins saw her as a great model of strength, and recalled in later years that his mother never seemed tired. Even though she had no more than an eighth grade education, a college education for her children was more important to her than anything except Mass on Sundays. During their brief time with a comfortable income, the Seitz family employed an African American maid. Mrs. Seitz pleaded with the woman to send her son to a Catholic school in Philadelphia, because she felt the education available to blacks in Delaware was inferior.

Except for the woman who worked for his family, Collins had little contact with African Americans growing up. No black families lived in his neighborhood and even though private schools did not have to follow the Constitutional requirement of separate schools (it only legally applied to public schools and other public places), his Catholic elementary school, St. Ann's, and all other private schools in Delaware obeyed the provision. So Collins never went to school with black children. Even his college, the University of Delaware, did not admit African Americans.

Each day, Collins' father drove the Seitz children as far as his workplace, and then the children walked the remaining three miles to St. Ann's. After school, they walked the three miles back to meet their father, and he drove them the rest of the way home.

In school, Collins was mischievous. Although he was very shy, and a bit of a loner, he enjoyed teasing the nuns. As a consequence, the nuns occasionally beat him for his antics. He was frequently sent to the pastor for misbehavior. Once, he stuffed the heater with paper, thinking the nun wasn't watching. She was. Another time, he and a friend changed the words to a Latin song they were singing in a solemn procession. They were supposed to sing the word "opranobus," and instead they sang, "Oh wipe your nobus." A nun, who was watching from the balcony, grabbed them by the backs of their necks, took them to the classroom, and beat them on the legs with a stick. She told Collins she would beat him until he cried. He refused to cry. (4)

Collins Seitz' St. Ann's yearbook photo, 1926.
Courtesy of St. Ann's School.

Life was very tense at home when Collins was young. His father was frequently ill during Collins' childhood, and when he was not ill, he was traveling for his job with the DuPonts. Margaret had to discipline and guide the children.

In 1929, when Collins was in the eighth grade, his father died. The family now had no income. Collins deeply resented that the DuPont Company had no provisions to take care of his mother. "They just washed their hands of you." (5)

DuPont was just like most companies. In those days, there was no social security, welfare or unemployment insurance. To make matters even worse, the economy plunged into a deep depression after the stock market crashed in October of 1929. During the Great Depression, as much as twenty-five percent of the people who wanted to work could not find employment.

The Seitz family plunged into poverty. They often did not have enough food or other necessities. At times, their electricity was turned off because they could not pay their bill. Collins' two oldest brothers were living on their own by now, so he and his other two brothers worked to support their mother. The Seitz boys took on a variety of jobs to help their mother keep the house. They developed a magazine distribution business, delivering magazines and newspapers to more than five hundred homes in Wilmington. One of Collins' deliveries was to an African American woman whom he fondly remembered years later. She had snow white hair, and she always invited him in for cookies and milk.

Franklin Delano Roosevelt was elected President in 1932, and his New Deal programs kept many families from hunger and homelessness. One of these programs enabled the Seitz's to keep their home. The New Deal kept the Seitz boys employed. Margaret was not only a devout Catholic, but also an avid supporter of FDR. Her children used to tease her, asking if she had to choose between Roosevelt and the Catholic Church, which would it be? She would just smile. They owed much to the New Deal.

Collins and the rest of his siblings finished their education in public schools because they could no longer afford the tuition for a Catholic high school. Collins spent his ninth grade year at a new junior high school, and then went on to graduate from Wilmington High School.

During his high school years, Collins separated himself from the shadow of his brothers. He and one of his brothers often clashed over politics and racism, and he viewed his older brother as closed-minded and overbearing. He had an English teacher whom he confided in and who guided him through some difficult times. "I was always bucking the establishment, and she was understanding...She was very, very nice and as I looked back she took a lot of nonsense from me." (6)

Collins graduated from high school in 1933 and was eager to go to college. He was admitted to the University of Delaware. Tuition was around two hundred dollars per year. His oldest brother was able to persuade the admissions office to accept a postdated check. Collins had little money, yet he was better off than most of his peers. Many of the students at the University of Delaware had no money and were malnourished.

Collins lived at home and drove to the university every day for four years in an old Chevy that had eighty-five thousand miles on it when he bought it for one hundred dollars. Most of the time, he didn't have enough gas to make the fifteen mile trip from Newark to Wilmington, so he often took a collection for fifteen cents to buy a gallon of gas so that he could get home. Students who could afford to, bought their meals at the cafeteria. Students who could not afford food stood outside waiting for the others to bring them food. Collins' mother made him peanut butter and jelly sandwiches each morning. Each evening, when he returned home, he and his brothers delivered magazines.

Collins continued to work a variety of odd jobs to help pay for college, including one job where he and his brothers traveled as far as New York City, dying cemetery grass green. He earned up to four hundred dollars per summer. One summer, he worked for a New Deal program which helped immigrants to become citizens. His job was to deliver diplomas to their homes. He did not know his way around Wilmington as well as his mother did, so she often accompanied him.

From the time he was a little boy, Collins knew that he wanted to be a lawyer. When he was still in elementary school, he used to sign his homework, "Collins J. Seitz, Attorney at Law." When he was in college, several experiences reinforced his career plans. One of these experiences was a logic class, which he loved. The course played a significant role in shaping his approach to legal problems. Collins was also on the debate team in college, and was thrilled by the competition and skill that was required to dissect his opponent's arguments.

One night, while he was still in college, he decided to attend a show at the Wilmington Playhouse. He was quite frugal with his money, and never attended shows, but the speaker was Clarence Darrow, one of America's most famous and most controversial attorneys at the time (and since). In one of his most famous cases, Darrow represented a biology teacher from Tennessee, named John Scopes who broke the law by teaching students about evolution in their science class. The state required that students learn creationism from the Book of Genesis in the Bible. Seitz was deeply impressed with Darrow's persuasiveness and logic, particularly when defending unpopular opinions. Collins experienced a life-changing moment that evening as he confirmed exactly what he wanted to do with his life. He decided he would apply to law school after he graduated from the University. Only one obstacle stood in his way. He had no money.

Collins Seitz' University of Delaware Yearbook photo, 1937. Courtesy of the University of Delaware Archives.

Chapter 5:
Vice-Chancellor Collins Seitz

"You will never be worth your salt if, at some time during your life, you don't take up a worthwhile cause and fight its fight." —Collins Seitz (1)

When Collins wanted to go to law school, the country was still in the middle of its worst economic crisis in history. Collins needed a scholarship to go to law school and so did most people who wanted to further their education. He was researching his options when he saw that the University of Virginia received a six million dollar grant from Philip Frances DuPont. He wrote to DuPont's widow and asked her for support. Time passed and he heard nothing. One day, while he was out cutting grass, his mother called him, telling him he had a phone call. Mrs. DuPont was on the phone. She wanted to interview Collins. He went to her home to see her. She was evidently impressed. She wrote a letter to the law school, recommending a scholarship and admission. In 1937, with his scholarship and two hundred dollars cash, Collins started law school at the University of Virginia. He said it was the greatest thing that ever happened to him.

In 1937, the Great Depression was in full swing. People were still hungry. A doctor at the University of Virginia stated that up to one-third of the entire student body was malnourished. Collins lived in a boarding house for ten dollars a month, and he lived mostly on a single meal a day of mashed potatoes, green beans and gravy. He hated green beans from that time on. All of Collins' money came from summer jobs. In his third year, he received an additional one hundred dollars toward his scholarship. He called this a "handsome increase." (2) The law school also loaned him money, which he paid back as soon as he was able after graduation.

Collins had his first experiences with racism when he was in law school. He witnessed two incidents which deeply disturbed him. In the first incident, he saw a white driver run a stop sign and hit a car driven by a black driver. The attending police officer arrested the black driver, even though it was clear to all observers that the white driver was at fault. The second event took place while he was riding on a segregated bus. A heavy-set older black woman got on the crowded bus and tried to make her way to the back of the bus where she was required by law to sit. She was carrying bundles, when teenagers on the bus began to push her around. She had difficulty reaching the back of the bus, and the white bus driver stopped the bus and taunted her. Collins gave her his seat.

When Collins graduated from law school in 1940, he knew only one lawyer in Wilmington. The lawyer, Stewart Lynch offered him a job practicing corporate law. He made one hundred dollars a month. Collins felt he got a great break with this job, because as soon as he started, Lynch was appointed United States Attorney for the District of Delaware. Lynch spent all of his time prosecuting and wasn't able to take care of his private practice. So Collins took over most of Lynch's practice, and argued his cases in the Court of Chancery where Seitz got to know the judges. He was in the court constantly, and quickly acquired skills and knowledge which took most lawyers many years to develop.

In 1943, Collins took a new job, working for a Wilmington corporate law firm, where his salary jumped from twelve hundred dollars per year to eighteen thousand dollars. This law firm was viewed as an "incubator of judges." (3) Collins also became active in the democratic party, and he took on the role of secretary for the New Castle County Democrats.

In 1946, Collins had yet another job change. The Chancellor at the Court of Chancery had become quite impressed with Collins' work. He wanted to make Collins the next vice-chancellor. In those days, the

Chancellor did the appointing. That was soon to change, but luckily for Collins, the state senate did not have to confirm his appointment—yet. The Court of Chancery was the highest court in the state. His job change made him the second highest ranking judge in Delaware—and at age 31, he became the youngest state judge in over a century. All types of cases were heard in this court, from copyright concerns to civil rights.

Although his hairline was receding, Collins looked much younger than his thirty-one years. His car had a license plate which said "judiciary" on it, and once, when he was parking his car, a police officer scolded him, pointing at his license plate, saying, "Young man, your father wouldn't like this." (4)

He still lived at home with his mother, but spent most of his time at work. He set aside little time to socialize. On a trip to Boston for a conference, he decided to listen to his mother's suggestion to stop in and see his brother in Kingston, New York. His brother had planned a boat trip with several friends. Collins told him he was too tired, but his brother insisted. One of the friends was Virginia Ann Day, an attractive and intelligent school principal from a small town in the Catskills. She was working on her master's degree at New York University, and she and Collins began a long-distance courtship that day. They courted for several years, and eventually were married in 1955. She was twenty-six and he was thirty-eight. They had four children within five years.

Collins admitted that he had a "love affair with the law" and was absent from home often. Even while Virginia was in labor, delivering the children, Collins was working on legal decisions out in the waiting room. Virginia was a patient and loyal partner, and she was as strong as Collins' own mother had been. Their marriage lasted over forty years, until Collins' death.

Shortly after Collins took the job of vice-chancellor, he met a Catholic priest who profoundly influenced his views on interracial matters. Father Thomas Reese spoke out passionately against racism. Reese believed that the Catholic Church and America's government needed to practice what it preached. Many people felt his beliefs were too radical. Collins said about Reese, "He was a dominant spirit in this community. He was the most amazing person. He could say the most profound things in a quiet way. And he would go to the legislature in Dover in the same way and they would beat on him and he would not retreat…" (5)

Reese founded the Catholic Interracial Council and persuaded Seitz and others to write monthly editorials on issues such as interracial marriage and the Catholic hospital's refusal to train black nurses. Collins even began participating on a local radio program, urging Delawareans to consider the meaning of such concepts as brotherhood, justice and equality. Tom Reese's guidance helped prepare Collins for the cases that he would soon face.

Chapter 6: Brooks Parker Versus the University of Delaware

"I just don't believe in a forbidden sign." —Helen Handy, plaintiff

In 1950, thirty-three black college students applied to the University of Delaware. When the university turned the students down for admission, Louis Redding took the case to the Court of Chancery. The case went before the vice-chancellor, Collins J. Seitz.

African American teenagers had few choices when it came to colleges, especially colleges in the south. In Delaware, there was only one college that accepted black students, Delaware State College, a historically black college founded in 1881, located in the center of the state.

White students in Delaware had more choices. Several private colleges only admitted white students, as did the University of Delaware, a flourishing public state university that had existed since 1743. In 1947, the university began admitting black graduate students to some of its programs, becoming the first southern state university to voluntarily admit blacks. But the University of Delaware's doors remained closed to black undergraduates.

By 1950, a wide gulf in quality existed between Delaware State College and the University of Delaware. Richard Kluger, a renowned author on the civil rights movement in education, called Delaware State College, "an academic shanty." (1) The college had four full professors and twenty-seven associate professors, whereas the university had forty-eight full professors and thirty-three associates. The faculty at Delaware State College made two-thirds the salary that the university professors made, and the college faculty had more classes to teach. The university had private study cubicles, and one hundred and forty thousand volumes in its neatly shelved, well-lit library. Delaware State College's library was originally designed as a chapel, and it housed only sixteen thousand books, most of which were piled on the floor because of limited shelf space. The college library had no study cubicles, and the lighting was dim, as one would expect in a chapel. The university had a health building, while the college had a doctor on call. Maids cleaned the dormitories at the university, while students did this work at the college. The university had a large selection of courses and state-of-the-art science labs. Delaware State College had no science labs and few course offerings. The university had swimming pools and gyms, the college had neither. The college received one-tenth the funding from the state that the university received. The University of Delaware had a beautiful campus with stately Georgian-style, red brick buildings with white columns and tree-lined sidewalks, while buildings and sidewalks seemed haphazardly placed at Delaware State College.

In 1944, the Middle States Regional Commission warned the college that it needed to make a number of improvements. Delaware State College received most of its funding from the state, but the state did not give the college additional money to make these improvements. Meanwhile, the state gave the University of Delaware adequate funding. As a result, in the late 1940s, Delaware State College lost its accreditation. Losing accreditation means losing recognition as a respectable institution. This meant that graduates of the college would have trouble getting into law school or medical school or any other type of graduate study.

In January, 1950, thirty-three black students from Delaware State College sent letters to the University of Delaware asking for applications in order to enroll in the fall. Brooks M. Parker was a senior at Delaware State College when he asked for an application to the University of Delaware. He actually had no intention of attending the university; he applied on principle. The case was eventually called *Parker versus University of Delaware* even though there were many other students involved. For example, Homer Minus was a sophomore who wanted to go into medicine, and the university could provide him with a level of training he would not get from the college. Helen Handy applied as a junior, saying, "I just don't believe in a forbidden sign." (2) It was clear to all the students that they were receiving an unequal education compared to the white students at the University of Delaware.

In the 1930's, the NAACP focused on improving education for black Americans within the segregated system. They challenged public universities and school systems throughout the country to meet the "equal" requirement of separate but equal. By the 1940's, they began challenging the "separate" aspect of the law. When Louis Redding decided to help Brooks Parker and the other students, his goal was to get them admitted to the white university, not to improve the black college.

Delaware State College and the University of Delaware were clearly separate and clearly unequal. Louis Redding and the NAACP encouraged the students to request the applications and to write letters explaining the accreditation concerns that they had. The admissions director at the university wrote back to the students explaining that Delaware State College is where black students go to college in Delaware. He did not send them any applications.

Louis Redding then wrote Judge Hugh Morris, the president of the university's board of trustees, and asked him to send application forms to the students. Judge Morris called a special meeting of the board to discuss Redding's request, but the board refused to change its segregation policy.

The university's board of trustees was a group of very prestigious and powerful men. The Governor was a trustee, as was the highest judge in the state, Chancellor Harrington of the Court of Chancery. Other judges and lawyers served, most of whom had graduated from the University of Delaware. Louis Redding was challenging much of the power and influence in the state when he decided to confront the university's board of trustees.

Ten of the original thirty-three students decided to pursue the issue, and with the help of Louis Redding and twenty-four year old Jack Greenberg, (a white attorney sent by the NAACP to assist Redding), they filed a lawsuit against the university. The students had two main arguments. First, they wanted a quality education, and Delaware State College was not providing an education equal to the university. Second, if the segregation policy were upheld, the students would be forced to attend colleges out of state, causing them a financial burden. The case ended up in the highest court in Delaware, the Court of Chancery.

At this time, the Court of Chancery had two judges—the Chancellor and the Vice-Chancellor. The Chancellor was William Watson Harrington, but he was a member of the university's board of trustees which meant he had a conflict of interest in the case. When a judge has a conflict of interest in a case, he or she is supposed to recuse—or remove him or herself from hearing the case. The case therefore fell to Vice-Chancellor Collins Seitz.

Redding intended to convince Seitz that any qualified African American student should be admitted to the university. If Redding succeeded, the University of Delaware would be the first university in the nation to be required to desegregate at the undergraduate level.

The interior of Chancery Court was surprisingly plain and simple considering the importance of the cases that were heard there. The court was sparsely decorated. No leather chairs, plush carpeting or elegant curtains adorned the small courtrooms. The windows in the court were left open in the summer, as the rooms could get quite stuffy. (Air conditioning was a rare luxury in those days.) Attorneys and witnesses often had to compete with the traffic outside the windows, and the rattling trucks always won the competition as they lumbered up the hill on 11th street in Wilmington.

Redding and Greenberg argued a strong case. They presented the two schools' course catalogues, the budgets and the testimony of many students. Redding argued that Delaware State College was inferior in every category: Facilities, faculty training, classroom equipment and curricula. He argued that if the State of Delaware denied these students access to a full and equal education at the University of Delaware, the state was in violation of the Fourteenth Amendment's guarantee of equal protection to all citizens, and therefore the state was breaking the law. Redding demanded admission for all qualified black students.

The state was represented by the state Attorney General, Albert James and the Deputy Attorney General, William Bennethum. Their job was to defend the University of Delaware. They argued that the case should be limited to these ten students rather than tried as a class action suit open to all qualified African Americans. They tried to convince Seitz, a University of Delaware graduate himself, that the university was really a private institution because it received a great deal of money in private donations. Private institutions are not held accountable to the Constitution the way public institutions are. The defense also argued that the college and the university were relatively equal.

African American students in many states were suing colleges and universities to allow them to attend. In some states, the courts threw out the cases, arguing that major differences did not exist. In other states, the courts told the universities or colleges to improve the black schools. Future students would benefit from the improvements, but not the group that filed the lawsuits.

Collins Seitz believed *Parker versus the University of Delaware* was an easy case. He did not order the university to enroll the ten students. His decision was broader than that. He argued that this case was a class action lawsuit, and not merely limited to these ten students. He said that the university was denying these students admission purely because of their race, and this created a "class." Second, he said the University of Delaware was clearly a public institution, receiving most of its money from taxpayers, and it therefore had to abide by the Constitution. The most remarkable part of his decision involved a visit to both campuses to see for himself the degree of difference between the two schools. He called the campus at the university, "a thing of beauty," whereas "one came away from the college with the feeling that... {it} was a most inadequate institution for higher learning." Seitz added that Delaware State College was "grossly deficient in every manner." (3)

Vice-Chancellor Seitz ruled that the University of Delaware could no longer consider color in its admissions. This was the first decision of its kind in the civil rights movement. The university could have appealed Seitz's decision to a higher court to try to change the decision, but they accepted it. The University of Delaware became the first southern university in the nation to desegregate.

Chapter 7: Backlash from the Senate

"I didn't oppose you because you're a Catholic, but because of your radical views." —Delaware state senator's statement to Collins Seitz

While most people in Delaware ignored Seitz's landmark decision in the case of *Parker versus University of Delaware*, many people throughout the nation paid close attention, especially African Americans. They were optimistic because not only did the Court decide in favor of the black plaintiffs, but also because the state did not appeal the Court's decision. The case set a precedent for later national arguments. For most Delawareans, a ruling involving a college or university had little impact on their lives, as most Delawareans did not attend college. Seitz's decision did, however, create significant changes in some of Delaware's communities. Some of the Catholic high schools in northern Delaware immediately began to admit black students, and the village of Arden, also in northern Delaware, integrated its elementary schools.

Besides the village of Arden, and the Catholic schools, one other group in Delaware paid particular attention to the Seitz decision: The State Senate. They made no secret over their displeasure with Seitz's decision in the *Parker* case. One year after the *Parker* ruling, Governor Carvel nominated Seitz for Chancellor—and he needed the Senate's approval.

Delaware had just created a supreme court, and Chancellor Harrington was appointed to this court, which left the Chancellor's position vacant. The only obstacle to Seitz's appointment was the Senate's confirmation. His earlier work with party politics was not going to help him.

Even though Seitz had worked for the Democratic Party, and even though the Governor was a Democrat and the majority of the Senate was Democrat (just barely, with nine Democrats and eight Republicans), getting confirmed was not going to be easy. As author Celia Cohen wrote, the Senate was "stubbornly segregationist" and they hated change. (1) Seitz knew that if he wanted to be confirmed, he should probably tone down his views, yet eleven days before his confirmation hearings took place, he gave an inspiring commencement address about racism to the graduating seniors at Salesianum High School, a Catholic high school in northern Delaware. The principal at Salesianum, Father Thomas Lawless, led the Catholic schools in integrating his school even before the *Parker* decision.

Seitz encouraged the students to have courage and conviction in a world that lacked both qualities. To illustrate his point, he asked, "How can we say that we deeply revere the principles of our Declaration and our Constitution and yet refuse to recognize these principles when they are applied to the American Negro…?" (2)

The confirmation hearing was supposed to take place at 2:00 p.m. on June 15, 1951. The Senate Democrats began with a private caucus. At 4:00 p.m., the Governor met with the Democrats while the Republicans went to dinner. After the meeting, the Democrats broke for dinner. Still no confirmation. Then everyone began to leave. Most high schools in the state were celebrating graduation during this weekend, and some senators were keynote speakers, while others had family graduations to celebrate. It was clear this was not going to be an easy vote, and the senators wanted to put it off. The Lieutenant Governor was supposed to speak at a graduation, but he was determined to make this vote happen, and he cancelled his speech. He decided to let the Republicans go, but he sent troopers to track down the Democrats and escort them back.

Meanwhile, the senators who had remained, were meeting with the Governor and the Secretary of State, probably making deals. One news columnist wrote that the administration promised to pave some roads in some districts in return for a vote for Seitz. (3) No one ever admitted to it, but the Governor later said, "I don't remember that, but it's not impossible." (4) Seitz never did learn whether any deals were made on his behalf.

Collins Seitz became the Chancellor at 1:25 a.m. on June 16th. All the Democrats and two Republicans voted. One senator later said to Seitz, "I didn't oppose you because you're a Catholic, but because of your radical views." (5) Another remarked, "We're supporting you for Chancellor, but I think you ought to know that there's feelings against you in the Senate because of your racial views." (6)

Collins Seitz receiving the oath of office as Chancellor from Justice Daniel Wolcott, June 19, 1951. Courtesy of the Seitz Family.

Chapter 8:
The Youngest Heroes and Heroines

"The timing had to be right. The issues had to be right. The arguments had to be right. The Plaintiffs had to be brave." (1)

Fifteen-year old Ethel Louise Belton wanted to go to the high school nearest her home. Ethel had a congenital heart condition that made her fifty minute trip to Howard High School exhausting. She walked many blocks and took several bus transfers. At the end of the school day, she walked nine and a half blocks to Carver, the vocational school to take a typing class because Howard High School did not offer typing classes. At the end of her school day, she made her long trek home. It was illegal for her to go to the high school nearest to her home, Claymont High School, because it was for white students only.

Seven-year old Shirley Barbara Bulah simply wanted to ride the school bus to her elementary school. Little Shirley's parents owned a farm and made their living selling produce and eggs to the community. Each day, Mrs. Bulah stopped her work on the farm to drive Shirley four miles roundtrip to school in an old, unreliable Chevrolet. Each day, a school bus drove by their farm taking white children to school #29 in Hockessin. The black school, #107C ("C" was for "colored"), was three blocks from the white school. Mrs. Bulah asked the bus driver to allow Shirley to ride the bus to the white school and then she could walk the rest of the way to #107C. The bus driver said Shirley could not ride the bus unless she went to #29. Mrs. Bulah said, "Then she will go to that school!" (2)

The town of Claymont in Delaware built its first school in 1805 and all the children who were able to attend school, both black and white, went to school together. In 1896, the Supreme Court decided in *Plessy versus Ferguson* that separate facilities were constitutional as long as they were equal. One year later, in 1897, the Delaware General Assembly wrote a new state constitution which included a section that called for separate schools for blacks and whites. The town of Claymont (and other towns) had to begin segregating the children in their community.

It is possible, at least in both the *Bulah* and *Belton* cases, if the state had spent more money trying to make the schools more equal, and if the state had provided bus transportation for the black students, these lawsuits might not have happened. These blatant inequalities easily outraged people. The psychological effects of segregation, however, were more subtle and difficult for most people to understand. Louis Redding wanted to emphasize both of these problems, the obvious inequalities between facilities, and the lasting traumatic psychological effects which segregation had on children.

Hockessin #29 was a four-room elementary school for white children, which had an auditorium, a basketball court, bus transportation, a well-equipped nurse's office, and beautiful landscaping. Hockessin #107C was a one-room schoolhouse with a divider that could be used to create two rooms. It had one toilet, a first-aid kit, no bus service and no landscaping. The children at 107C received tattered, discarded hand-me-down books from the white school The books had missing pages, and students had to share books when they were completing their work, in case one of the pages was missing from their own book.

When Mrs. Bulah went to Lawyer Redding for help with her school bus concern, Redding told her he would not take the case if all she wanted was a ride on the white bus in order to go to the black school. He said, "If you go all the way, I'll take the case. Don't be like so many others that start and then stop." Mrs. Bulah replied, "I'm here for the duration." (3) This case became known as *Bulah versus Gebhart*. Gebhart was a member of the State Board of Education.

When the new Howard High School was first built in the 1920s, it was one of the finest schools in the region. By 1952, Howard remained in relatively good condition, but was still surrounded by old industrial buildings and poor housing. The vocational wing at Carver was embarrassingly inferior to Howard. Claymont, the white high school, was built on fourteen acres with playground equipment and plenty of room for sports. The state recommended a ratio of twenty-five students to each teacher, and while some classes at Claymont had more than twenty-five students, every class at Howard and Carver was overcrowded. Claymont offered more courses, and students did not need to leave the building to attend any classes.

Seven other teenagers joined Ethel Belton to apply for admission to Claymont High School. The school board turned them down, telling them the state law forbade black children to go to school with white children. A family member of one of the board members recalled that members of the Claymont Board of Education actually encouraged the students to apply, knowing the children would be denied admission but hoping the black families would challenge the rejection in court. The board members believed that was the only way to get the law changed. (4) This case became known as *Belton versus Gebhart.*

As soon as Redding filed the lawsuit, the state quickly made changes to Hockessin #107C. They installed water fountains, fixed the bathroom, and upgraded the playground equipment. They would not, however, provide a bus. The Bulahs refused to drop their lawsuit.

People were much more emotional about the *Bulah* and *Belton* cases than the University of Delaware case. Few people attended college, whereas everyone attended their neighborhood school. Schools were often the center of the community. Schools were places where people gathered for pot luck dinners, shows, bingo, and town meetings. Schools were where children shaped their identities and developed lasting friendships. When people talked about integrating the neighborhood school, emotions ran high.

As the lawsuits became public, white customers stopped going to the Bulah's farm. Their business collapsed. Even black members of the community taunted the family. One teacher said to Shirley, "I don't know why your mother is doing this. We don't want change at 107." Her classmates at 107C pulled her hair and stole her books. (5) Just as the Beltons before them, the Bulahs also refused to back down.

Chapter 9:
An Historic Decision

"The application of Constitutional principles is often distasteful to some citizens, but that is one reason for Constitutional guarantees. The principles override transitory passions." —Collins Seitz

Louis Redding combined the *Bulah* and *Belton* cases and presented them together because each case involved the same questions about constitutionality and equality, and he was seeking the same solution in each case. He intended first, to convince the judge that segregation was unconstitutional because it violated the students' right to equal protection under the Fourteenth Amendment. And second, he hoped to prove that the current education offered in the segregated system was terribly unequal.

Attorneys argued the same points in four similar cases around the nation (Virginia, South Carolina, Kansas and Washington D.C.) In all four cases, the judges ruled that discrimination and inequality were not intentional, and where it existed, the school districts needed to improve the unequal schools. Each court upheld the principle of separate but equal, and in each case, the black children lost. People throughout the nation watched the Delaware case with great interest. The judge for the Delaware case was Collins Seitz.

Attorney General H. Albert Young and Deputy Attorney General Louis Finger represented the State of Delaware, arguing that segregation did not violate the Fourteenth Amendment and that no substantial inequality existed between the white schools and the black schools.

Jack Greenberg joined Louis Redding again, and together they brought many expert witnesses to testify about the effects that segregation had on children. They used experts in education, sociology, psychology, psychiatry, and anthropology. Jerome Bruner, an education professor from Harvard, presented evidence that segregation produced apathy, frustration and hostility in black children. One of the nation's most well-known and highly respected psychiatrists, Frederic Wertham, testified that segregation created inner conflict within black children which affected their mental health. He pointed out that the impact varied from child to child, and conceded that segregation alone didn't necessarily create these problems. Dr. Wertham offered the metaphor, "If a rosebush should produce twelve roses and if only one rose grows, it is not a healthy rosebush. It is up to us to find out what is interfering with its growth and with its health." (1)

He went on to argue that since a democratic government enforced this particularly hurtful law, the government sent a message to black children that they were unfit to learn in the same classroom as white children. Wertham said segregation brought about a lack of interest, and excessive absenteeism for black children. And worst of all, segregation made black children feel inferior, and left white children feeling superior. One white child in Wertham's experiment said that kids in her class wanted to tie up black children and make them work. "The boys say that they [the black children] should work and we should play." (2)

Another famous expert was Kenneth Clark who had carried out an experiment with forty-one black children from Delaware. In his experiment, he showed the children a white doll and a black doll and asked them questions. He informed Chancellor Seitz that, "three out of four youngsters—who when asked that question, 'Which of these dolls is likely to act bad?' picked the brown doll...Now you see when 100 percent of these youngsters correctly identify themselves with the brown doll...I think we have clear cut evidence of rather deep damages to the self-esteem of these youngsters." (3)

The state did not present any witnesses to challenge these experts. The Attorney General argued that the state of Delaware was not ready for black and white children to go to school together. He argued that this was a social problem—a problem of attitudes which the law would not be able to change. He said that a legal solution to a social problem was no solution. The law could not force people to feel differently. The most the Court could do, he argued, was to order that the black schools be equalized, brought up to par with the white schools.

Redding and Greenberg had done a meticulous job, but they were worried. The attorneys who argued the four other national cases had also done outstanding work, yet they all lost their cases. There had been signs in the four earlier cases, however, that the system was beginning to crack. For example, in two of the cases, some judges disagreed with the majority opinion and wrote dissenting opinions where they explained why they agreed with the black plaintiffs. But the majority of the judges ruled to keep segregation intact.

Collins Seitz had to decide on these questions of historic significance. The pressure was intense. Public feelings against integration ran high. He received so many threats that police officers stood on duty in his driveway throughout the court proceedings. On April 1, 1952, he delivered his decision.

First, in response to the Attorney General's argument that Delaware was not ready for desegregation, Chancellor Seitz pointed out that this argument ignored the effects that segregation was having on black children. In addition, he wrote, "The application of Constitutional principles is often distasteful to some citizens, but that is one reason for Constitutional guarantees. The principles override transitory passions." (4)

Once again, Seitz personally visited the white schools and the black schools. In his decision, he gave a detailed description of the differences between the schools, concluding that the facilities available to black children were substantially inferior. The Attorney General had anticipated that it would be difficult to convince anyone that the schools were equal, so his argument rested on equalizing the schools. During his presentation, he pointed out that there were plans underway to improve the offerings at Howard, to build a new black high school a few miles south of Howard to ease overcrowding, and that Hockessin had already made improvements to 107C.

Seitz disagreed with the Attorney General's argument. He gave three reasons. First, he said the Attorney General did not address the psychological effects of segregation. Second, the Court did not have authority over the building of schools. His third reason was particularly noteworthy:

> [T]he U.S. Constitution has been violated. It seems to me that when a plaintiff shows to the satisfaction of the Court that there is an existing and continuing violation of the 'Separate but Equal' doctrine, he is entitled to…the State facilities which have been shown to be superior. To do otherwise is to say to such a plaintiff: 'Yes, your Constitutional rights are being invaded, but be patient, we will see whether in time they are still being violated.'…[S]uch a plaintiff is entitled to relief immediately…To postpone such relief is to deny relief, in whole or in part, and to say that the protective provisions of the Constitution offer no immediate protection. (5)

All of the other states had accepted the argument that the schools should be given time to equalize. Seitz rejected this argument with these historic words, but they were only half of his decision. Even more significant was his opinion regarding the Separate but Equal law itself, and his challenge to the United States Supreme Court. He reviewed how he had been asked to decide whether separate schools could ever be equal even though all arguments supporting *Plessy* implied that separate could be equal. He wrote that his own Court of Chancery "does not believe such an implication is justified under the evidence…I believe the 'Separate but Equal doctrine in education should be rejected." (6)

Collins Seitz was a devout believer in the Constitution which established a federal system of government, granting many responsibilities to the states and providing the structure of the federal government, including the duties of each branch, which is why he added:

> I do not believe a lower court can reject a principle of U.S. Constitutional law which has been adopted…by the highest court of the land…I…believe its rejection must come from that Court…
> …I, therefore, conclude that while State-imposed segregation in lower education provides Negroes with inferior educational opportunities, such inferiority has not yet been recognized by the United States Supreme Court as violating the Fourteenth Amendment…It is for the Court to re-examine its doctrine in the light of my finding of fact. (7)

The dissenting judges in the other national cases had agreed that segregation hurt the self-esteem of black children, and that separate therefore could not be equal, but Collins Seitz took the next step of issuing the challenge to the highest court in the nation. Collins Seitz was suggesting that the United States Supreme Court should overturn the *Plessy versus Ferguson* decision!

This was the first time that a court had ordered a segregated public school to desegregate. Thurgood Marshall, the lead attorney for the NAACP and the first African American to eventually serve on the United States Supreme Court, said of Seitz's decision, "This is the first real victory in our campaign to destroy segregation of American pupils in elementary and high schools." (8)

Claymont High School became the nation's first public high school to integrate in the south. It was not easy for the brave teenage pioneers to suddenly attend the formerly all white high school. There was name-calling and shoving at times. But these teenagers believed that creating the opportunity for future children was worth it.

Little Shirley Bulah was warmly welcomed on her first day at Hockessin 27. Her teacher introduced her to the class and told her to pick any desk she wanted.

The Seitz decision and his challenge to the Supreme Court laid the foundation for what many legal scholars and historians suggest was the most important case in twentieth century America.

Chapter 10: Brown Versus Board of Education, Topeka, Kansas

"Probably no case ever to come before the nation's highest tribunal affected more directly the minds, hearts, and daily lives of so many Americans." —Richard Kluger *(1)*

Redding and Greenberg were thrilled that Seitz had ruled in their favor, but they realized they won primarily on the grounds that the schools were not equal. They were hoping to outlaw the entire practice of segregation. What they needed now was for the case to be appealed all the way to the United States Supreme Court so that the Supreme Court could abolish segregation once and for all. It was a risk. What if the Supreme Court decided that Seitz was wrong? Yet, the time felt right. They knew it was now or never.

The Delaware State Board of Education immediately appealed Seitz's decision to the recently created Delaware Supreme Court, but the new court upheld the decision eight days before the new school year began, just barely in time to integrate the schools that were part of the *Bulah* and *Belton* cases. The State Board of Education learned that the four cases that had been argued in other parts of the nation had been appealed to the United States Supreme Court, and they decided to appeal their case as well, which was exactly what Redding and Greenberg had hoped for.

The United States Supreme Court combined the cases from Kansas, Virginia, South Carolina, the District of Columbia, and Delaware, and used the Kansas case as the title: *Brown versus Board of Education, Topeka, KS.* Linda Brown was an African American child in Kansas who wished to attend the white school close to her home. She lost her case. The children in Virginia, South Carolina and Washington, D.C. also lost. The state courts had all ruled against the plaintiffs (the children) and the plaintiffs appealed their cases up to the Supreme Court. Delaware had the only case in which the plaintiffs won, and so it was Delaware's state school board who appealed to the Supreme Court.

Louis Redding was well aware of the extraordinary opportunity he now had to present a case to the United States Supreme Court. Few lawyers ever have such a chance. The majestic corridors of the United States Supreme Court, and its cathedral high ceilings and marble columns seemed a world away from the simple architecture and noisy courtrooms of Delaware's Chancery Court. But Louis did not allow himself to be intimidated by these surroundings.

The Supreme Court listened to the first round of arguments in mid-December, 1952. The NAACP strategically laid the groundwork with these cases. Each case presented separate arguments. Redding and Greenberg argued their cases last. The lawyers for the other cases had already made the constitutional arguments, so Redding and Greenberg kept their presentation short. When the two Delaware attorneys finished, the first phase of the case was over.

The chief justice was Fred Vinson. In the oak-paneled conference room, he led the discussions among the other eight justices. Their opinions were split. Several resisted the idea of overturning the *Plessy* precedent. Many of the school districts had ordered that the schools be equalized, and some of the justices wanted to allow enough time to see if equalization worked. Chief Justice Vinson was not passionate about either side, but he was worried that a sweeping decision outlawing segregation might cause serious problems. Many states had made it clear that regardless of the Court's opinion, segregation would continue. They believed a ruling that outlawed segregation would violate states' rights. The judges who favored desegregation feared that a bare majority of five to four would send a weak message to a divided nation. Supreme Court decisions are often split, but the feeling on both sides was that the decision in this case needed to be strong and clear. Either segregation was constitutional or it wasn't. By June, 1953, the judges were still split, and the chief justice was reluctant to push for a decision.

Justice Felix Frankfurter decided that the lawyers should appear for a second round of arguments. He wanted the lawyers to specifically present answers to three questions: What impact did the original writers of the Fourteenth Amendment think the amendment would have on public education? Second, was it within the power of the judiciary to abolish segregation, or did this power belong to a different branch of government? And third, if the power did belong to the judges, how could the court have its decision carried out?

Tragedy struck just before the second round of arguments was to begin in October of 1953. Chief Justice Vinson died of a heart attack. The attorneys for both sides panicked. The impact of a new justice and a new chief justice would be dramatic. Each side thought they knew where each justice stood on segregation, and the attorneys knew what kinds of arguments worked with each justice. They also knew that Fred Vinson would not have tried to force a particular decision either way. A strong new justice could make the difference for either side.

The Constitution outlines how a Supreme Court judge is selected, dividing the job between the executive and the legislative branches. The President selects a candidate and Congress votes whether to confirm that choice. President Dwight D. Eisenhower, a Republican, chose the Governor of California, Earl Warren (also a Republican) for the job of Chief Justice. Eisenhower wanted someone with character and ability, who would inspire confidence in the public. The President wanted someone who was moderate in his views, who would be confirmed by both democrats and republicans. Dwight Eisenhower believed Earl Warren fit these criteria.

The President thought Warren was fair, hardworking, smart enough but not brilliant, easygoing and likely to be moderate on controversial issues. Warren had one significant controversial stain on his record. During World War II, after the Japanese had bombed Pearl Harbor, it was Earl Warren's idea to round up Japanese Americans who lived on the West Coast and relocate them to camps in the desert for the remainder of the war. Warren regretted this act toward the end of the war, agreeing that focusing on Americans of Japanese decent had been both racist and unnecessary.

A second area of concern for the civil rights lawyers was Warren's strong support for states' rights. The strongest legal argument for segregation was that the Constitution clearly left questions of education up to the states. Louis Redding was fairly certain that a governor who favored states' rights and who supported the Japanese American internment would never vote to take away state control of segregation by race. Redding was not optimistic.

Chapter 11: A Unanimous Decision

"Our Constitution has no provision across it that all men are equal but that white men are more equal than others." —James Nabrit, attorney for D.C. plaintiffs

Congress eventually confirmed Earl Warren's appointment to the Supreme Court, but not until after the second round of arguments in *Brown* had begun. Warren hastily moved from California to Washington, D.C. so that he could hear this case and he immersed himself in all that had been written and presented up to that point.

The second round took three days to present. Seated in black leather swivel chairs, the nine justices listened from the enormous bench overlooking the podium from which the attorneys presented their arguments. The attorneys began with the question of what the framers of the Fourteenth Amendment thought the amendment's impact would be on public education. Both sides argued that the history was inconclusive. Some records indicated that the Fourteenth was specific in its application, while other records showed the amendment as very general.

The second question was whether the Court had the constitutional power to overturn segregation laws. The NAACP argued that the Fourteenth Amendment directly and clearly prohibited discrimination and therefore segregation. Eighty-year old John W. Davis was one of the attorneys arguing for South Carolina against desegregation laws. He argued eloquently that the emotions surrounding issues of race could not be denied. He warned that the Supreme Court could not act as a "glorified board of education" and that the Court needed to trust that ultimately the states would do the right thing for children of all races. (1)

Justin Moore, the attorney for Virginia argued that Jim Crow laws had served both races well, and to argue otherwise showed a lack of understanding of the South and its history. A third attorney insisted that with the help of white people, former slaves had made great progress, and the Supreme Court should not disturb this.

Thurgood Marshall, however, insisted that the only way the Supreme Court could continue to allow "separate but equal" was if the nine justices believed that blacks were inferior. "[N]ow is the time, we submit, that this Court should make clear that that is not what our Constitution stands for." (2) James Nabrit, an attorney for the plaintiffs in the D.C. case said, "Our Constitution has no provision across it that all men are equal but that white men are more equal than others." (3)

The United States Assistant Attorney General, J. Lee Rankin, spoke as a friend of the Court. He stated that the Department of Justice agreed that "segregation in public schools cannot be maintained under the Fourteenth Amendment." (4)

The third question was how to carry out desegregation if the Court did find that segregation was unconstitutional. The Assistant Attorney General said the cases should be sent down to the district courts to work out the process, and schools could have one year to formulate their own plans. Several of the justices were very concerned with this plan. They predicted that some school districts would refuse to carry out the courts' orders, or that some courts would procrastinate.

Earl Warren was quiet throughout the proceedings. The Court adjourned mid-afternoon on December 9, 1953. Attorneys for both sides immediately began hypothesizing which justices were on their side. None of the attorneys knew where Earl Warren stood on these questions, but his opinion became immediately clear to the eight other Supreme Court justices. As they convened to discuss the case, he explained that he felt it was a simple case which had one clear answer. The question though was how to shape the decision.

Earl Warren agreed with Thurgood Marshall that "separate but equal" could continue only if the Court decided that African Americans were inferior, and Warren knew none of the justices could make that case. The justices agreed that no race is inferior. Since this was true, the Chief Justice concluded that segregation had to end.

Warren wanted the decision to be unanimous. A five to four decision or any other split was unacceptable. He wanted a united court. Not all justices agreed with him, however. Stanley Reed argued that as long as the separate schools were made equal, states needed to decide for themselves if and when to desegregate. Robert Jackson believed that ending segregation was a political decision, a creation of a new law, which was not the job of the Supreme Court.

The other justices generally agreed with Warren, with some reservations. Felix Frankfurter struggled with the legal history and precedents, but believed that desegregation would best serve justice. William Douglas agreed with Warren and said the Court should decide on the basic principle and worry later about how to integrate schools. Harold Burton had made up his mind early to oppose segregation. Tom Clark feared a violent reaction if the Court's decision were not handled carefully. He agreed with desegregation but wanted each state to decide for itself how to carry it out. Sherman Minton believed that the country had changed a great deal since *Plessy* and it was time to end segregation. Hugo Black also agreed that segregation must end.

Seven justices favored ending segregation, but even the seven were not united. They disagreed on the basic issue as well as how much detail and direction the decision should give. Earl Warren was determined to get a decision that everyone could agree to. He decided the group should not rush the decision. Instead, they would discuss various aspects of the case over the next few weeks at lunch and in meetings, as a whole group, and in smaller groups. Robert Jackson and Stanley Reed were the two major holdouts.

By February, Jackson continued to struggle with how to justify ending segregation from a judicial standpoint. The courts had upheld segregation for decades all the while insisting the Constitution permitted segregation. Jackson believed the Constitution neither supported nor opposed segregation, although he did conclude that the interpretation of the Constitution could legitimately change from age to age. Jackson felt that the wrong branch of government was being asked to end segregation. He saw desegregation as a legislative duty. His clerk, however, convinced him that if the public believed the decision was based on certain truths about equality and black progress and the Constitution, people would accept the decision. Jackson was persuaded, and joined the majority.

Stanley Reed, meanwhile continued to work on his dissenting opinion. He felt that the Equal Protection Clause did not guarantee completely equal public facilities. He agreed with Jackson that public policy fell under the legislature's job description, not the judiciary's. He felt the nation had made great progress in race relations and he feared a decision banning segregation could halt the progress. Reed and Warren continued to meet and discuss the case. In the end, Reed decided that in spite of these obstacles, he had to consider what was best for the country, and his conscience told him segregation was wrong. He decided to vote in favor to end segregation, but he insisted that integration be allowed to occur gradually.

At 12:52 p.m., May 17, 1954, every newsroom in the country was listening as Earl Warren explained that the opinion he was about to read was unanimous. At first, listeners could not tell which way the decision was going. The Chief Justice spent twenty minutes describing the background of the cases and explaining the Court's understanding of the Fourteenth Amendment and how the Court had interpreted *Plessy* over time. Then he explained how much more important public education had become compared to a century ago.

> "Today, education is perhaps the most important function of state and local governments...It is the very foundation of good citizenship...In these days, it is doubtful that any child may reasonably be expected to succeed in life if he is denied the opportunity of an education. Such an opportunity...is a right which must be made available to all on equal terms."

He continued, saying that separating children

> "...solely because of their race generates a feeling of inferiority as to their status in the community that may affect their hearts and minds in a way unlikely ever to be undone...Any language in Plessy versus Ferguson contrary to this finding is rejected.

At 1:20, he reached the end of the decision, saying,

> ...We conclude that in the field of public education, the doctrine of 'separate but equal' has no place. Separate educational facilities are inherently unequal. (5)

Louis Redding was driving his car when he heard the news over the radio. He had to pull over to catch his breath and let it sink in. "Oh boy, terrific!" he whispered. (6)

Collins Seitz said, "It is a matter of great satisfaction to me that my judgments were the only ones affirmed by the Supreme Court...More to the point, the United States had come somewhat closer to keeping faith with its Declaration of Independence." (7)

Louis Redding, Irving Morris (a Delaware civil rights lawyer), and Jack Greenberg. Courtesy of The News Journal Company, 9/30/98. Photographed by Fred Comegys.

Chapter 12: Changed Lives

"They were courageous pioneers blazing trails through controversial and then uncharted territories of law and justice which ultimately brought to our state the true meaning of justice for all."

The desegregation cases deeply affected the careers and lives of Louis Redding and Collins Seitz. Throughout the *Brown* case, threats were "rather routine" for the Seitz family. Virginia Seitz, Collins' wife, bravely insisted that the presence of threats "...wasn't a big deal. It just wasn't that important." (1)

The next step up the career ladder for Seitz would logically be to serve on the state's Supreme Court, which had replaced the Chancery Court as the highest court in the state. After the *Bulah* and *Belton* cases, many of Seitz's colleagues agreed that he had destroyed his career when he made such "radical" decisions. (2) Seitz never saw it that way. As it turned out, in 1966, President Lyndon B. Johnson appointed Seitz to the Third U.S. Circuit Court of Appeals. He later served as the chief judge for the Third Circuit for thirteen years. He remained with the court as a senior judge until he died at the age of 84.

Redding's life was even more dramatically affected by the *Brown* case. He often received hate mail, and once, someone even drove him off the road. During the two years that he worked day and night preparing for *Brown*, in addition to taking on cases for the African American community, he fell behind in his accounting. He had never been a particularly careful record keeper. In these years, his wife gave birth to three children, and his father had a stroke. Louis let a number of important recordkeeping responsibilities slip. He failed to renew his driver's license, he forgot to update his insurance to cover his growing family, and he missed the deadline for paying his income taxes.

It is fair to say that Louis was overwhelmed by his work and family responsibilities. Self-employed professionals are supposed to pay their taxes four times a year and Louis paid his sporadically. The Internal Revenue Service (IRS) filed charges against Louis claiming that he willfully failed to pay his income taxes. Four Delaware attorneys were indicted for failing to pay their taxes, but only Louis's name was made public. If he were convicted, he could go to jail and lose his license to practice law. He was forced to defend himself in court. His lawyer, Ned Carpenter, a white attorney from northern Delaware took Louis's case. Carpenter told the jury, "He was a man leading an unusual life. I wish it would have been possible for you to have seen him in his office in 1953 or 1954 eating lunch at his desk while working, dictating, or working at night in the library or on weekends. Was he forming a plan to commit an evil? He was a man who could not say no, especially to the needs of his race at a crucial time in its history." (3) The twelve jurors, after over two hours of deliberation, rendered their verdict: Not guilty! Everyone in the courtroom cheered. The normally reserved Louis Redding wept.

That was not the end of Redding's legal troubles. A "red scare" was sweeping the country. Fear of communism dominated the political culture. The red scare meant that anyone who was accused of being a communist or had ever been a member of the communist party, could lose their job and their reputation. Joseph McCarthy, a senator from Wisconsin, convinced many Americans that communists were lurking at all levels of government. The House Un-American Activities Committee (HUAC), a congressional group which held hearings about supposedly disloyal and unpatriotic actions, focused their attention on Louis Redding. They alleged that Redding had communist ties, that he was "as red as his name." (4). HUAC tried to discredit many civil rights leaders by accusing them of communist influence. They even spied on Martin Luther King, Jr.

The Federal Bureau of Investigation (FBI) had been monitoring Louis's activities closely. They even went through his mail. One day, when Louis was busier than he ever thought possible, preparing for the Brown case, the FBI stopped him on a stairway. They pressured him to agree to talk to them and they questioned his communist connection. He told them that some of his anti-segregation efforts may have been construed as communist party activities, but added, "That depends on who is construing the activity." (5) Louis Redding was disgusted by these charges, reminding his accusers that his work revolved around exposing and destroying discrimination, and nothing else. The FBI kept his file open, but HUAC eventually dropped the investigation.

Eventually life settled down for both men. Redding's practice and reputation grew. Seitz spent the rest of his life as a judge, but remained active in his community. He became concerned about poverty and how poor people did not have the same kind of access to justice as people who could afford to hire lawyers. He helped establish the Community Legal Aid Society, a legal services organization which provides free legal help to poor people, elderly people, and people with disabilities.

Both Louis Redding and Collins Seitz died within one month of each other in the fall of 1998. Their work forced America to come closer to living up to the ideals set out in the Declaration of Independence and the Constitution. Today, this is recognized and commonly accepted. Fifty years ago, it was not.

The journal for the Delaware State Bar Association wrote about Seitz and Redding, "They were courageous pioneers blazing trails through controversial and then uncharted territories of law and justice which ultimately brought to our state the true meaning of justice for all." (6)

Delaware State Bar Association mourns the death of two of Delaware's legal giants. They were courageous pioneers, blazing trails through controversial and then uncharted terrain of law and justice, which ultimately brought to our State the true meaning of justice for all.

November 1998 • Volume 22, Number 4

Bulk Rate
U.S. Postage
PAID
Permit No. 249
Wilmington, DE

Cover of *INRE: The Journal of the Delaware State Bar Association*, November, 1998—one month after the death of both Redding and Seitz. Courtesy of the Delaware State Bar Association.

Chapter 13: The Turning Point

"I'm not too upset if the glass is half full. At the time of Brown, it was completely empty. Maybe in far less than fifty years, it will be completely full." —Jack Greenberg

The *Brown* decision gave courage and hope to many Americans. The decision's impact was immediate and dramatic Seven months after the Supreme Court delivered its decision, Rosa Parks and the NAACP made national news when they challenged segregation on the busses in Montgomery, Alabama. Martin Luther King, Jr., at the age of twenty-seven, became the spiritual leader of the Montgomery Bus Boycott which then launched the Civil Rights Movement. African Americans led boycotts and sit-ins against segregated lunch counters. College students, black and white, risked their lives registering black people in the south to vote.

Many school districts quietly opened the doors for black children. Other schools closed down in protest. Even districts within states disagreed over how and when to begin integration. Many districts took years to integrate, and did so only after the government threatened to de-fund them unless they desegregated.

Today, tens of thousands of schools throughout the nation are integrated. Delaware has one of the most integrated school systems in the country, and Delaware's minority students score higher on national tests than the national average. (1) Delaware State College is now called Delaware State University and boasts a beautiful campus with a wide variety of degrees and course offerings available to students of all races.

When Louis Redding was young, only about one-tenth of black families were middle class. Today, close to one-third of all black families are middle class. (2) It is not unusual for an African American to run for a major political office and get elected. Today, there are many black military leaders, lawyers and doctors. The culture is more accepting of interracial marriage and interracial adoption.

Serious problems remain, however. Although de jure segregation (segregation required by law) no longer exists in the United States, many schools in the nation are still segregated (de facto segregation). Poverty among African Americans is far greater than among whites. Unusually high unemployment rates for black Americans, as well as crime in the inner cities contribute to the poverty. Most black children are raised by single mothers. The murder rate among black men is ten times that of the rest of the population. Many people argue that rap music and videos reinforce stereotypes and create tensions. (3)

At a fiftieth anniversary celebration of the *Brown* decision, held at the University of Delaware in the spring of 2004, an elderly Jack Greenberg, the attorney who began his career with Louis Redding in the public school cases, responded to this uneven progress by saying, "I'm not too upset if the glass is half full. At the time of Brown, it was completely empty. Maybe in far less than fifty years, it will be completely full." (4)

Brown versus the Board of Education was a turning point for America. Racism still exists, but thanks to *Brown*, it is not officially supported by the law. Children who attend schools where there is diversity have more interracial friendships, hold fewer racial stereotypes, feel more comfortable with peers of different races, and often choose to work in multicultural settings. (5)

Annette Woolard-Provine, who wrote her doctoral dissertation about the Redding family, once asked Louis Redding what he thought about the complaint that America still has race problems. Redding answered, "Young lady, if there are wrongs that still need to be righted, someone should be working on that." (6)

Endnotes

Chapter 1

(1) Richard Kluger, *Simple Justice* (New York: Random House, 1975), p. 444
(2) Collins Jacques Seitz, interview by A. Leon Higginbotham, Jr., 21 February 1986, Center for the Study of Civil Rights, Carter G. Woodson Institute for Afro-American and African Studies, University of Virginia, Charlottesville, VA

Chapter 2

(1) Annette Woolard-Provine, *Integrating Delaware: The Reddings of Wilmington* (Newark: The University of Delaware Press, 2002) p. 21
(2) ibid, p. 52
(3) ibid, p. 50
(4) Annette Woolard-Provine, p. 60, quoting from *The News Journal,* 24 November 1985

Chapter 3

(1) Annette Woolard-Provine, *Integrating Delaware: The Reddings of Wilmington* (Newark: The University of Delaware Press, 2002), p. 91, quoting from *Sunday Bulletin,* (Philadelphia), 27 February 1977
(2) ibid, p. 90

Chapter 4

(1) Margaret Seitz, interview by author, 3/16/04.
(2) Collins J. Seitz, interview by A. Leon Higginbotham, Jr., 4 May 1993, transcript by The Historical Society of the United States Court of Appeals for the Third Circuit, p. 12
(3) ibid, p. 14
(4) ibid, p. 11
(5) ibid, p. 15
(6) ibid, p. 18

Chapter 5

(1) Collins J. Seitz, Sr., Speech to Graduating Class of Salesianum High School, 5 June 1951
(2) Ned Carpenter, "A Conversation with Judge Collins J. Seitz, Sr.", *Delaware Lawyer,* Fall, 1998, p. 24
(3) Celia Cohen, *Only in Delaware: Politics and Politicians in the First State* (Delaware: Grapevine Publishing, 2002), p. 55
(4) ibid, p. 55
(5) Ned Carpenter, "A Conversation with Judge Collins J. Seitz, Sr.", p. 26

Chapter 6

(1) Richard Kluger, *Simple Justice* (New York: Random House, 1975), p. 289
(2) Annette Woolard, "Parker v. University of Delaware: The Desegregation of Higher Education in Delaware." *Delaware History,* Fall/Winter, 1986, p. 115
(3) Parker v. University of Delaware, 75 A.2d 225, Court of Chancery of Delaware, New Castle, September 9, 1950

Chapter 7

(1) Celia Cohen, *Only in Delaware: Politics and Politicians in the First State* (Delaware: Grapevine Publishing, 2002), p. 57
(2) Collins J. Seitz, Sr., Speech to Graduating Class of Salesianum High School, 5 June 1951
(3) Celia Cohen, *Only in Delaware: Politics and Politicians in the First State,* p. 58 citing from William P. Frank, *Bill Frank's Delaware,* (Middle Atlantic Press Inc., 1987), p. 285
(4) Celia Cohen, *Only in Delaware: Politics and Politicians in the First State,* p. 58
(5) ibid, p. 58
(6) ibid, p. 57

Chapter 8

(1) Beth Miller and James Merriweather, "After Desegregation, Students Endured an Ugly New World," *The News Journal,* 17 May 2004, p. A7

(2) Sean O'Sullivan, "Delaware Family Endured Hardship to Fight Lawsuit," *The News Journal,* 17 May 2004, p. A6
(3) ibid
(4) Virginia Smiliack and Evelyn Tryon, *Claymont: A Story Never Told, A Recognition Never Given.* (AARP Meeting, Claymont, DE) 14 September 1995
(5) Sean O'Sullivan, "Delaware Family Endured Hardship to Fight Lawsuit," *The News Journal,* 17 May 2004, p. A6

Chapter 9

(1) Richard Kluger, *Simple Justice* (New York: Random House, 1975), p. 444
(2) ibid, p. 443
(3) ibid, p. 440
(4) Belton et. Al. v. Gebhart et. Al., Bulah et. Al. v. Gebhart et. Al., Civ. A. Nos. 258, 265, Court of Chancery of Delaware. New Castle. April 1, 1952
(5) ibid
(6) ibid
(7) ibid
(8) Richard Kluger, *Simple Justice*, p. 449

Chapter 10

(1) Richard Kluger, *Simple Justice* (New York: Random House, 1975), p. x

Chapter 11

(1) Richard Kluger, *Simple Justice* (New York: Random House, 1975), p. 672
(2) ibid, p. 674
(3) ibid, p. 677
(4) ibid, p. 675
(5) Brown v. Board of Education, Topeka, 347 U.S. 483, 1954
(6)Annette Woolard-Provine, *Integrating Delaware: The Reddings of Wilmington* (Newark: The University of Delaware Press, 2002), p. 126
(7) Celia Cohen, *Only in Delaware: Politics and Politicians in the First State* (Delaware: Grapevine Publishing, 2002), p. 60

Chapter 12

(1) Virginia Seitz, telephone interview with author, 23 March 2004
(2) Ned Carpenter, telephone interview with author, 30 November 2004
(3) CeliaCohen, *Only in Delaware: Politics and Politicians in the First State* (Delaware: Grapevine Publishing, 2002), p. 62, quoting from *Morning News,* 2 December 1956
(4) Carl Weiser, "Guilty Only of Heroism," *The Sunday News Journal,* 19 December 1999, p. A1
(5) ibid
(6) *INRE: The Journal of the Delaware State Bar Association,* "Delaware State Bar Mourns the Death of Two Legal Giants," November, 1998, vol. 22, #4, cover

Chapter 13

(1) Michelle Fuetsch, "State's Minority Students Excel," *The Sunday News Journal*, 16 November 2003, p. A1
(2) Annette Woolard-Provine, *Integrating Delaware: The Reddings of Wilmington* (Newark: The University of Delaware Press, 2002), p. 19
(3) Beth Miller and Mike Chalmers, "Black Delawareans' Opportunities Grow," *The News Journal,* 19 January 2004, p. A1
(4) Jack Greenberg, keynote speaker at *The Redding Symposium of Brown,* University of Delaware, 23 April 2004
(5) Beth Miller, "Attorney, Judge Played Key Roles," *The News Journal,* 17 May 2004, p. A6
(6) ibid

Photograph Credits

(1) Louis Redding's Brown University yearbook photo, 1923, courtesy of Brown University Archives
(2) Collins Seitz' St. Ann's yearbook photo, 1926, courtesy of St. Ann's School
(3) Collins Seitz' University of Delaware Yearbook photo, 1937, courtesy of the University of Delaware Archives.
(4) Collins Seitz receiving the oath of office as Chancellor from Justice Daniel Wolcott, June 19, 1951, courtesy of the Seitz Family.

(5) Louis Redding, Irving Morris, and Jack Greenberg, courtesy of The News Journal Co. 9/30/98. Photographed by Fred Comegys.
(6) Cover of *INRE: The Journal of the Delaware State Bar Association*, November, 1998—one month after the death of both Redding and Seitz, courtesy of the Delaware State Bar Association.
(7) Photograph of the author by R. Eric Young—www.YoungsStudio.com. August 31, 2007.

Bibliography

Books

Cohen, Celia. *Only in Delaware: Politics and Politicians in the First State.* Delaware: Grapevine Publishing, 2002.

Hess, Debra. *Thurgood Marshall: The Fight for Equal Justice.* New Jersey: Silver Burdett Press, 1990.

Kluger, Richard. *Simple Justice.* New York: Random House, 1975.

Woodward, Bob and Scott Armstrong. *The Brethren.* New York: Simon and Schuster, 1979.

Woolard-Provine, Annette. *Integrating Delaware: The Reddings of Wilmington.* Delaware: University of Delaware Press, 2003.

Periodicals

Allen, William T. "The Honorable Collins J. Seitz: Greatness in a Corporate Law Judge." *Delaware Lawyer.* Fall, 1998.

Batchelor, Jennifer. "Collins J. Seitz, Sr: A Man Ahead of His Time." *Delaware Law Weekly.* 5/12/04.

Carpenter, Ned. "A Conversation with Judge Collins J. Seitz, Sr." *Delaware Lawyer.* Fall, 1998.

Carroll, Beatrice Patton. "Leonard L. Williams." *Delaware Lawyer.* Summer, 1998.

The Delaware State Bar Association. "Delaware State Bar Association Mourns the Death of Two Legal Giants." *INRE: The Journal of the Delaware State Bar Association.* November 1998, vol. 22, #4.

Halberstam, David. "Brown v. Board of Education: What It Means to Every American." *Parade.* 4/18/04.

Landman, James. "An End and a Beginning: The Fiftieth Anniversary of Brown v. Board of Education." *Social Education.* January/February, 2004.

Morris, Irving. "The Role of Delaware Lawyers in the Desegregation of Delaware's Public Schools: A Memoir." *Widener Law Symposium Journal.* Vol. 9, Issue 1, 2002.

Seitz, Collins, Jr. "Tribute of a Son." *Delaware Lawyer.* Fall, 1998.

Seitz, Virginia A. "Chancellor Seitz's Perspective on Brown v. Board of Education." *Delaware Lawyer.* Spring, 2004.

Sloviter, Dolores K. "Collins J. Seitz, An Unparalleled Colleague." *Delaware Lawyer.* Fall, 1998.

Williams, Leonard L. "Louis Redding." *Delaware Lawyer.* Summer, 1998.

Woolard, Annette. "Parker v. University of Delaware: The Desegregation of Higher Education in Delaware." *Delaware History.* Fall/Winter, 1986.

Newspapers

Chase, Randall. "Delawareans Look Back on Brown." *Delaware State News.* 5/17/04.

Fuetsch, Michelle. "State's Minority Students Excel." *The Sunday News Journal.* 11/16/03.

Miller, Beth. "A Shared Passion for Equal Justice." *The News Journal.* 5/17/04.

Miller, Beth. "Attorney, Judge Played Key Roles." *The News Journal.* 5/17/04.

Miller, Beth and Mike Chalmers. "Black Delawareans Opportunities Grow." *The News Journal.* 1/19/04.

Miller, Beth and James Merriweather. "After Desegregation, Students Endured an Ugly New World." *News Journal.* 5/17/04.

Miller, Beth and James Merriweather. "Delaware Cases First in Nation to Strike Down Desegregation Law." *The News Journal.* 5/17/04.

Nagengast, Larry. "Brown versus Board Part of Judge's Legacy." *The Dialog.* 5/13/04.

Nagengast, Larry. "Judge Sent Message in Speech to '51 Graduates." *The Dialog.* 5/13/04.

O'Sullivan, Sean. "Delaware Family Endured Hardship to Fight Lawsuit." *The News Journal.* 5/17/04.

Parra, Esteban. "Commemoration of Color in Claymont." *The News Journal.* 11/19/97.

Weiser, Carl. "Guilty Only of Heroism." *The Sunday News Journal.* 12/19/99.

Interviews

Carpenter, Ned. Telephone interview with author. 30 November 2004.

Seitz, Collins and William Poole. Videotaped interview for the Community Legal Aid Society, Inc. Wilmington, DE, 15 April 1996.

Seitz, Collins Jacques. Interview by The Honorable A. Leon Higginbotham, Jr., 21 February 1986. Center for the Study of Civil Rights, Carter G. Woodson Institute for Afro-American and African Studies, University of Virginia, Charlottesville, VA.

Seitz, Collins J., Sr. Interview by The Honorable A. Leon Higginbotham, Jr. 4 May 1993. Transcript, The Historical Society of the United States Court of Appeals for the Third Circuit.

Seitz, Margaret. Telephone interview with author. 16 March 2004.

Seitz, Virginia. Telephone interview with author. 23 March 2004.

Speeches

Greenberg, Jack. Keynote Speaker at *The Redding Symposium of Brown.* University of Delaware. 23 April 2004.

Seitz, Collins J., Sr. Speech to Graduating Class of Salesianum High School. 5 June 1951.

Seitz, Virginia A. Eulogy for Collins J. Seitz, Sr. 21 October 1998.

Smilack, Virginia and Evelyn Tryon. *Claymont: A Story Never Told, A Recognition Never Given.* AARP Meeting, 14 September 1995. Claymont, DE.

Other Publications

P.S. DuPont and African American Schools in Delaware. Delaware: Hagley Museum and Library. 2004.

Court Cases

Belton v. Gebhart (and Bulah v. Gebhart), 87 A.2d 862 (Del. Ch. 1952).

Brown v. Board of Education, Topeka, 347 U.S. 483, 1954.

Parker v. University of Delaware, 75 A.2d 225, Court of Chancery of Delaware. New Castle. September 9, 1950.

Videos

A Separate Place (The Schools P.S. DuPont Built). Delaware: Hagley Museum and Library. 2004.

Additional Recommended Reading

Cottrol, Robert J., Raymond T. Diamond and Leland B. Ware. *Brown v. Board of Education: Caste, Culture, and the Constitution.* Kansas: University Press of Kansas. 2003.

Greenberg, Jack. *Crusaders in the Courts: Legal Battles of the Civil Rights Movement.* New York: Twelve Tables Press. 2004.

Ogletree, Charles J. *All Deliberate Speed.* New York: W.W. Norton and Company. 2004.

Recommended Web Sites

www.delrec.org (Delaware Law Related Education Center)

www.jimcrowhistory.org

www.splcenter.org (Southern Poverty Law Center)

www.tolerance.org